PRAISE FOR THE 1 CORINTHIANS

M000118920

Lori and Becky effectively blend scriptural principles and real life examples into both books in *The 1 Corinthians 13 Parent* series. Each page is a mirror that will reflect the reader's parenting strengths and challenges. Parents, be encouraged…you are not alone. You will be helped in this invaluable calling. I highly recommend The *1 Corinthians 13 Parent* books to anyone looking to evaluate, tweak, or implement a spiritually-based parenting plan.

-Kirk Weaver, Family Time Training
Founder and Executive Director

These are excellent books. *The 1 Corinthians 13 Parent* series has a great idea. It takes a new spin on a common passage and applies it to the family. It's fresh. It's new but it's based in the Scripture. People will love the idea. This is a winner in my opinion.

-Dr. Scott Turansky, National Center for
Biblical Parenting and author

In *The 1 Corinthians 13 Parent* series, Lori Wildenberg and Becky Danielson display not only a heart for children, but an insightful passion to help parents consider the primary place of influence they hold in the development and formation of their kids. Throughout the books, the authors highlight key points of learning and offer key questions, as well as suggestions intended to give parents the right tools to raise their children to love, honor, and respect both God and others. The books serve as a reminder that God is love and that parents have the awesome privilege and responsibility to reflect that love to their children. The authors remind us that parenting is a holy calling and not to be taken for granted. Read, reflect, and learn!

-Reverend Mark R. Stromberg, Superintendent of the
Northwest Conference of the Evangelical Covenant Church of America

In a time when parents have a tendency to feel inadequate and believe they are just hanging on, both books in *The 1 Corinthians 13 Parent* series is a breath of fresh air. These books give us powerful principles, real-life examples, and a clear path to success. Not just books to read, but to study and let them take you on a journey that will make you a better parent and a better person. Every church should use these resources for small group study for parents of children of all ages.

-Dr. Chuck Stecker, President of A Chosen
Generation, Author, Speaker and Ministry Leader

THE 1 CORINTHIANS 13 PARENT

RAISING LITTLE KIDS WITH BIG LOVE

STUDY GUIDE

THE 1 CORINTHIANS 13 PARENT

RAISING LITTLE KIDS WITH BIG LOVE

LORI WILDENBERG
BECKY DANIELSON M.ED.

Bold Vision Books
PO Box 2011
Friendswood, Texas 77549

ISBN# 978-0-9912842-5-2

Published in association with Books & Such Literary Management, 52 Mission Circle, Suite 122, PMB 170, Santa Rosa, CA 95409-5370 www.booksandsuch.com

Printed in the United States of America.

Cover photograph by Michael Scneidmiller

Interior and Cover created by kae Creative Solutions

Edited by Deb Strubel, Katie McDivitt

Bold Vision Books
PO Box 2011
Friendswood, Texas 77549

CONTENTS

INTRODUCTION

LOVE IS HEART WORK

Love is patient, love is kind.
It does not envy, it does not boast, it is not proud.
It is not rude, it is not self-seeking, it is not easily angered,
it keeps no record of wrongs.
Love does not delight in evil but rejoices with the truth.
It always protects, always trusts, always hopes, always perseveres.
Love never fails.

1 Corinthians 13:4-8a

Families that flourish are grounded in unconditional love, love with no strings attached. Let's take a closer look at the day-to-day behaviors of toddlers and youngsters that make a flourishing family challenging. I think you'll agree with Lori and me: Parenting is not for the faint of heart. Each parent, child, and relationship is unique. There is no set formula. Parenting is fluid and creative. We are thankful that God's Word is living and active so we can apply its principles to parenting.

The expectations we have for ourselves and our children play out in the way we raise our little kids. Acknowledging the fact that there is only one perfect parent—God—and only one perfect son—Jesus—gives us a good, healthy start. As humans we all mess up, parents and youngsters alike. Love truly does cover a multitude of sins.

This supplemental manual is the companion to *1 Corinthians 13 Parent: Raising Little Kids with Big Love*. It has been designed to further assist and guide you in applying the concepts discussed in the book. Our prayer is that the tips, strategies, and techniques presented will encourage and equip you while you raise your little one. The questions are meant to move you from reflection to action. An answer key is provided in the back of this booklet for your convenience.

Each chapter in this manual corresponds to a chapter in the book. After the opening element(s) in each chapter in this workbook, you will encounter three separate questions with the headings *Reflect*, *Relate*, and *Refocus*.

♥ The Reflect questions will assist you in contemplating what you have read in the book. Sometimes you may need to refer back to the book to find answers.

♥ The Relate questions will aid in applying the previous Reflect principles.

♥ The Refocus component will prepare you to parent with intentionality from a Christian perspective.

Start by taking the two assessments that follow: the Family of Origin Assessment and the Parent Assessment. The assessments will help you determine (1) how your past may be influencing you today and (2) where you are today in the realm of quality parenting.

Next, go to the Parenting Styles Chart, which describes different approaches and helps you discover your default parenting style. As you reflect, relate, and refocus, be prayerful. Ask the Lord to open your eyes and heart to parent and love in the *most excellent way* according to 1 Corinthians 13.

IF I HAVE FAITH THAT CAN MOVE MOUNTAINS, BUT HAVE NOT LOVE, I AM NOTHING.

1 Corinthians 13:2b

FAMILY OF ORIGIN ASSESSMENT

1. Growing up, how were mistakes handled in your family (frustration, blame, patience, etc.)?

2. How was faith taught and lived in your family of origin?

3. Who made the major decisions in your home?

4. How would you describe the type of discipline your father used (train, punish, ignore, etc.)?

5. How would you describe your mother's approach to discipline?

6. How would you characterize your relationships with your siblings?

7. How was conflict dealt with in your family?

8. How were emotions expressed (freely, with restraint, repressed, etc.)?

9. What positive things would you like to pass along to your children from your upbringing?

10. What negative patterns from your upbringing would you like to change or avoid?

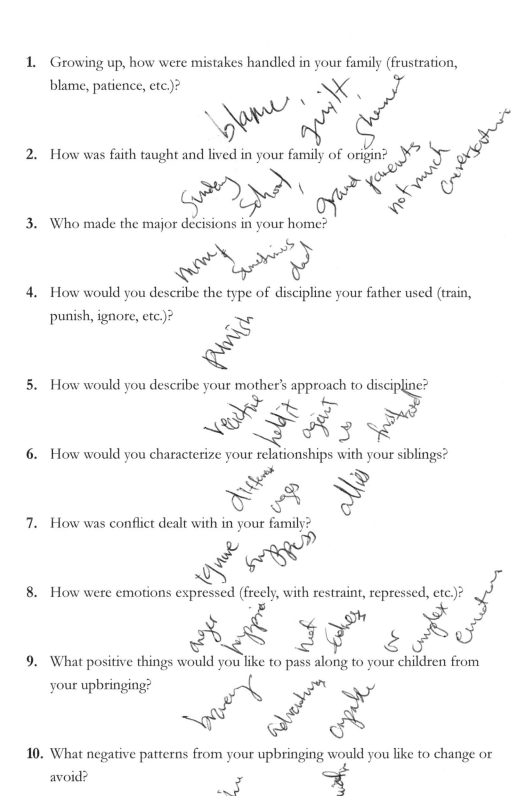

REFLECT

Take a few moments to evaluate the results of your Family of Origin Assessment. What are your strengths? What are your weaknesses?

RELATE

Compare and contrast your parenting techniques to that of your parents. Thank God for the positive traits you received from your family of origin. Ask the Lord to help you move past generational sins and forgive where needed.

REFOCUS

What strategies from the past are worth keeping? What areas need adjustment? What needs to be abandoned?

Next, take the Parent Assessment that follows. This assessment isn't a scientific evaluation but a tool to stimulate thought and discussion.

PARENT ASSESSMENT

As you read each statement below, give it a number that corresponds to how well you believe you do or how much you agree with each item. Please use your first impression.

1. Not Yet
2. Just Started
3. Halfway There
4. Mostly Developed
5. In Place

__4__ I adjust my discipline techniques according to my child's age, stage, and personality.

__3__ I avoid speaking for my child.

__5__ Each family member is strongly committed to the family.

__5__ I encourage sibling relationships.

__1__ I resist the urge to compare one child to another.

__4__ I effectively deal with undesirable behavior, like lying or stealing.

__3__ Respect permeates the home.

__4__ Responsibilities are shared.

__3__ I don't punish my children because of my anger.

__5__ My family shares an attitude of forgiveness.

__4__ I attempt to understand the reasons behind my child's behavior.

__5__ My family supports one another in difficult times.

__3__ I arm my children with strategies to help during tempting moments.

__5__ Family mealtimes are a priority.

__4__ I teach my children right from wrong using God's Word, the Bible.

__3__ A common bond of faith is important in my family.

__3__ I am able to work effectively with my child's teachers.

__3__ Appreciation for one another is demonstrated.

__3__ Clear family guidelines for technology and media are stated.

__3__ Screen time (computer, TV, iPod, etc.) is limited in our home.

__2__ Priorities are clearly defined.

__5__ There's a sense of humor and play in the home.

__4__ Crises are dealt with by turning to God and family members for support.

__5__ Leisure time is spent together as a family.

__5__ My family believes each person is created for a purpose.

13

REFLECT

What are you doing well? What areas need to be addressed?

RELATE

Compare your answers with your spouse's responses. It is very likely you will see things differently. Use this assessment as a vehicle for discussion.

REFOCUS

Set goals in the areas you and your spouse want to improve. For example, if mealtimes are not a priority, commit to eating together as a family two to three times a week.

The 1 Corinthians 13 Parent
Raising Little Kids with Big Love

Parenting Styles

To better help you determine your dominant parenting style, read through the list below. Choose one statement that best describes how you currently parent your child.

1. "I'll help you." (Parent's motivation is to train and be with child.)

2. "Oh, I'll do it for you; you have other things to do." (Parent's motivation is to be considerate of child.)

3. "Do it this way." (Parent's motivation is for the job to be done correctly.)

4. "Do whatever you want." (Parent's motivation is to be uninterrupted.)

5. "Do you want help?" (Parent's motivation is to respect child's needs.)

6. "I'll do it myself." (Parent's motivation is to get the job done quickly.)

Now match the number you chose above to the description below to discover your parenting approach.

Parent Style	Positive Result	Negative Child Result
Chum	Models helping out	May take advantage of no responsibility
Controller	Job is done right	Feels inadequate
Consultant	Child feels respected	May need more guided practice
Coach	Good bonding time and training	May not want or need help
Clueless	Child is totally responsible	Feels abandoned and unappreciated
Checked Out	Parent gets job done	Missed opportunity to learn/bond

1 Corinthians 13 Parent: Raising Little Kids with Big Love
Parenting Styles Chart

RELATIONSHIP-BASED CHILD-FOCUSED

The Chum
"I want to be my child's best friend."

Values:	child's happiness, friendship with parent
Parent Behavior:	high degree of warmth, acceptance, responsive, undemanding, indulgent, indecisive, weak, power relinquished, rescues, unable to say no, whines, begs, pleads, highly involved, makes excuses for child
Fear:	conflict, doesn't want child to get upset
Discipline Strategy:	permissive
Negative Result:	child is dependent, disrespectful, whiny, manipulative, demanding, insecure, resentful
Positive Result:	child feels loved, knows he belongs

THE CONSULTANT
"I'M HERE TO ADVISE."

VALUES:	child's decision-making skills, maturity, independence
PARENT BEHAVIOR:	actively observes, listens, evaluates, imparts wisdom when asked, may ask permission to give advice
FEAR:	wonders if child is ready for this. Asks self, "Have I said too little or too much?"
DISCIPLINE STRATEGY:	allows natural consequences to be the teacher, asks questions
NEGATIVE RESULT:	child may flounder and make lots of mistakes
POSITIVE RESULT:	child is independent, responsible, confident, knows parent is there for support

THE CLUELESS
"I BLINDLY TRUST MY CHILD."

VALUES:	child's independence and maturity
PARENT BEHAVIOR:	overwhelmed or stressed, weak, warm, relies on belief child is always good, unable to keep promises, uninformed, relies heavily on others to help raise child, undemanding, appears laid back, confused, blames others for child's behavior, feels helpless
FEAR:	"I won't know what to do, or I'll be more overwhelmed if I engage."
DISCIPLINE STRATEGY:	threatens but ultimately does nothing, avoids discipline
NEGATIVE RESULT:	child is rebellious, angry, prone to aggressive behavior, disrespectful, seeks structure, doesn't feel capable
POSITIVE RESULT:	child may become a risk-taker and is resourceful.

THE CONTROLLER
"I'M IN CHARGE."

VALUES:	order and good behavior
PARENT BEHAVIOR:	forceful, decisive, highly organized, controlling, demanding, overbearing, micro-manager, authoritarian, highly involved, points, preaches, threatens, instills guilt, takes over
FEAR:	loss of control, lack of respect
DISCIPLINE STRATEGY:	punishment
NEGATIVE RESULT:	child is dependent, resistant, rebellious, withdrawn, blames others, lies, sneaky
POSITIVE RESULT:	child feels safe and secure

THE COACH
"I'M HERE TO GUIDE AND LEAD."

VALUES:	family unity, rules, interdependence, cooperation, commitment, connection
PARENT BEHAVIOR:	encourages and supports child in struggles, provides solutions, sets limits, authoritative, responsive, demanding, actively involved, able to make the tough call
FEAR:	loss of family unity
DISCIPLINE STRATEGY:	prevention, training, retraining, redirecting
NEGATIVE RESULT:	child may lose some autonomy and individuality due to the family focus
POSITIVE RESULT:	child feels capable, lovable, secure, accountable, responsive, respectful, cooperative

THE CHECKED OUT
"I'M BUSY."

VALUES:	own personal time and schedule
PARENT BEHAVIOR:	busy, workaholic, distracted, may try to buy love with material items, unattached or disconnected, strong-willed parent, cold , uninvolved, unavailable, self-absorbed
FEAR:	child will be dependent
DISCIPLINE STRATEGY:	none unless a big problem, then jumps to extreme punishment
NEGATIVE RESULT:	child is withdrawn, seeks attention from other adults, may try to prove worth through achievement, defeatist attitude, doesn't feel loved
POSITIVE RESULT:	child is self-reliant and resourceful

REFLECT

What is your typical style, the one you generally fall back on in most interactions with your child? (Note: With young children the Consultant approach is not recommended as a main strategy.)

RELATE

Why would it be beneficial to use various parenting styles?

REFOCUS

How can you include some elements of each of the four desirable parenting styles listed below into your parenting?

(Note: With young children you are more likely to be highly involved and your default style probably will be Chum or Controller. Intentionally balance your approach with elements of opposite non-default style.)

Chum:

Controller:

Consultant:

Coach:

Pray for a balance in relationship and rules as you parent your child.

AND NOW I WILL SHOW YOU THE MOST EXCELLENT WAY.

1 Corinthians 12:31

Chapter 1

Choose Patience

Love is patient.

1 Corinthians 13:4a

Patience is easier with some children than others, and tougher with your own! (Having been classroom teachers and then moms, Becky and I can say a hearty "Amen" to that statement.) When annoyed, embarrassed, inconvenienced, or challenged by our children, it is difficult to be patient. But patience, like any other virtue, is a choice. The goal is to become a patient parent and model this trait. Patience is a matter of the will, a choice.

Review the Family of Origin Assessment. Were your mom and dad patient? Growing up in a household where patience reigns typically reproduces patient people. But if this quality wasn't present, it will need to be developed. The Bible tells us to dress ourselves in patience (Colossians 3:12b). Patience is the foundational trait of love. It is a virtue we want to pass on to our children.

Therefore, as God's chosen people, holy and dearly loved, clothe yourselves with compassion, kindness, humility, gentleness and patience.

Colossians 3:12

REFLECT

Is *patient* a word you would use to describe yourself? Why? Why not?

What have past parenting circumstances caused you to lose your patience?

What situations trigger impatience in your child?

RELATE

How will you handle times when impatience and frustration stir in you?

Do you have difficulties with specific times of day or situations: mealtime, bedtime, and potty training? Write out a plan to tackle the problem.

In what situations do you allow your youngster to make some choices?

REFOCUS

When is it difficult for your child to wait?

How will you help your child strengthen his "wait" muscle?

Using the Bible concordance as a guide, find and record verses that pertain to patience.

PRAY COLOSSIANS 1:9B-12 FOR YOUR CHILD.

> Lord Jesus, I have not stopped praying for (child's name) and asking you to fill (child's name) with the knowledge of your will through all spiritual wisdom and understanding. And I pray this in order that (child's name) may have a life worthy of you and may please you in every way: bearing fruit in every good work, growing in the knowledge of you, being strengthened with all power according to your glorious might so that (child's name) may have great endurance and patience. Amen.

A MAN'S WISDOM GIVES HIM PATIENCE;
IT IS TO HIS GLORY TO OVERLOOK AN OFFENSE.

Proverbs 19:11

Chapter 2

Choose Kindness

Love is kind.
1 Corinthians 13:4b

Paul wrote, "Be kind and compassionate to one another" (Ephesians 4:32). Kindness is the attribute that binds families together. Without it, families can easily be torn apart. Kindness includes gentleness, empathy, compassion, and helpfulness. Good manners are a form of kindness, too. Parents set the tone in the home. When we display a kind attitude in words and actions, family blessings multiply.

How would you describe the atmosphere in your home? Is it a place where kindness is shown? If not, the strategies in this chapter will further guide you in reclaiming kindness in your family. Begin with one small act of kindness and watch it grow!

Encourage one another and build each other up.
1 Thessalonians 5:11a

Reflect
How was the attribute of kindness portrayed in your family as a child?

When you experience unkind words or actions, how do you react?

Does kindness reign in your home or has the environment become riddled with sarcasm and impatience?

RELATE

Has the teasing in your home turned from fun to hurtful? How will you address the situation?

What is your plan to extinguish inappropriate physical behaviors like hitting, pinching, and biting?

What jobs could your child do to be a little helper, teaching him to value kindness through service?

REFOCUS

How can authentic praise encourage your child? How can insincere praise hurt a child?

Mark your calendar to include play in your day. We bless our kids when we give them the present of our presence.

USE ISAIAH 63:7 TO PRAY FOR THE LOVING-KINDNESS GOD HAS PROVIDED FOR YOUR CHILD.

> Lord, grant that I will tell of the kindnesses of the Lord, the deeds for which you are to be praised, according to all you have done for (child's name), yes, the many good things you have done for (child's name), according to your compassion and many kindnesses.
> Amen.

**THE LORD APPEARED TO US IN THE PAST, SAYING:
"I HAVE LOVED YOU WITH AN EVERLASTING LOVE;
I HAVE DRAWN YOU WITH LOVING-KINDNESS."**

Jeremiah 31:3

CHAPTER 3

CHOOSE CONTENTMENT

LOVE DOES NOT ENVY.

1 Corinthians 13:4c

Contentment is serenity, satisfaction, pleasure, and gratification all rolled into one. The opposing trait is envy, the green-eyed monster who suddenly appears when expectations are not met. The things we desire are here today and gone tomorrow, temporary in the grand scheme of things. Yet we envy those who have what we want.

Controlling the green-eyed monster is tough. Helping children determine the difference between a want and a need is helpful. But the best tactic for parents is to model gratitude and contentment. Remember, as the anonymous saying goes, "The happiest people don't have the best of everything. They just make the best of everything they have." Be grateful for the gifts the Lord has provided.

A HEART AT PEACE GIVES LIFE TO THE BODY, BUT ENVY ROTS THE BONES.

Proverbs 14:30

REFLECT
How are you affected by the trap of materialism?

Was keeping up with the Joneses part of your family life as a child?

"True contentment with _____ one is and with _____ one has creates joyful satisfaction."

RELATE

Has purchasing gifts for others been an issue for your child? If so, how can you make the shopping experience different next time?

What are the six steps to help siblings disengage before squabbles escalate?

1. _____

   .

2. Ask each child to come up with a positive solution or approach to the dispute.

3. Have each child _____
   _____.

4. Encourage a compromise, incorporating parts of both plans if possible.

5. Have the kids present their plan to _____
   _____.

6. Allow the kids to come to a _____
   _____ and _____ their plan.

REFOCUS

What will you do if your child takes something that doesn't belong to him?

As a family, make a list of blessings to encourage thankfulness and contentment.

PRAY JOB 36:11 FOR YOUR CHILD.

Lord, may (child's name) obey and serve you, spending the rest of his days in prosperity and his years in contentment.
Amen.

FOR YOU MAKE ME GLAD BY YOUR DEEDS, O LORD;
I SING FOR JOY AT THE WORKS OF YOUR HANDS.

Psalm 92:4

CHAPTER 4

CHOOSE HUMILITY

LOVE ... DOES NOT BOAST, IT IS NOT PROUD.

1 Corinthians 13:4

In Scripture, humility is welcomed while pride is despised. In society today, the opposite is true. The prideful people are in the spotlight and the humble are ignored. But in all truthfulness, wouldn't you rather spend time with humble rather than boastful friends? Humility draws others in. Pride pushes them away.

Humility is a noble trait to instill in our children. We desire to have our children possess a healthy self-image and so we praise them when appropriate. But we want the praise to be sincere and realistic. Pride often begins with comparisons, believing one is better than another. Correction coupled with encouragement is a healthy combination. As Christian parents, our job is to address issues of pride and to humbly lead our children. Pride glorifies self while humility glorifies the Lord.

LET HIM WHO BOASTS BOAST IN THE LORD.
2 Corinthians 10:17

REFLECT
How can you follow Paul's advice in Romans 12:3: "Do not think of yourself more highly than you ought, but rather think of yourself with sober judgment"?

When you are faced with correction or criticism, how do you react, with anger, indifference, or thankfulness?

When you praise your child, is it accurate and sincere or over-the-top inflating? How can you modify your words?

RELATE

In what areas of your child's life could the combination of correction plus encouragement inspire him?

What small things can your child do well to merit praise?

How can sharing the credit bring graciousness, cohesiveness, and humility into your home?

REFOCUS

What tactics can you use to teach good sportsmanship to your child?

How will you apply the concept "correction is not rejection" when retraining your child?

PRAY THE WORDS OF PHILIPPIANS 2:3-4 FOR YOUR CHILD.

Lord, may (child's name) do nothing out of selfish ambition or vain conceit, but in humility consider others better than himself.
Amen.

WE KNOW THAT WE ALL POSSESS KNOWLEDGE.
KNOWLEDGE PUFFS UP, BUT LOVE BUILDS UP.

1 Corinthians 8:1b-c

CHAPTER 5

CHOOSE RESPECT

LOVE IS NOT RUDE.

1 Corinthians 13:5a

Is there anything worse than a rude little kid? Well, perhaps a rude adult! Disrespect is definitely an issue in our society today. Lack of respect is at the core of rudeness. Going against the tide and expecting respect is a Christian parent's duty. That means training our children and perhaps retraining ourselves. A respectful attitude is a choice.

In children, disrespect is usually manifested in uncooperative behavior and disobedience. The tips and strategies in this chapter will help you raise the bar in the respect arena. Scripture tells us in Proverbs 21:21, "He who pursues righteousness and love finds life, prosperity and honor." Love is teaching your children to be respectful.

MY SALVATION AND MY HONOR DEPEND ON GOD; HE IS MY MIGHTY ROCK, MY REFUGE.

Psalm 62:7

REFLECT
Are you respectful to others?

Does your language honor God, or do you use the Lord's name casually?

Describe ways you have expected and enforced respectful behavior from your child.

RELATE

If obedience is desired, don't ask a _____, don't whine, and don't bargain. Issue a _____, and be ready to move.

Are manners a priority for your family? If not, what can you do?

What are some tactics you can use to decrease your child's dawdling?

REFOCUS

What are the steps for gaining cooperation?

1. _____ _____ prior to an event. This is positive prevention. "Hang onto the cart when we are in the grocery store" (Controller).

2. _____ while the event is occurring and mention the family value to be reinforced. "Remember, hang onto the cart while we are in the store so we can stick together" (Controller/Coach).

3. _____with a stated _____ if the child isn't obeying. "Hang on or you'll have to get in the cart. To be safe we stick together" (Controller).

4. _____ _____with the stated consequence if the child doesn't obey the instruction. "In the cart you go. This will keep you safe" (Controller).

5. _____ is the final step. Parent's choice. Try to make it fit the crime.

How can you model honoring your parents and in-laws to teach your children the value in respecting their elders and others?

PRAY PSALM 119:168 FOR YOUR CHILD.

May (child's name) obey your precepts and your statutes, for all (child's name) ways are known to you.
Amen.

WHEN I CONSIDER YOUR HEAVENS, THE WORK OF YOUR FINGERS,
THE MOON AND THE STARS, WHICH YOU HAVE SET IN PLACE,
WHAT IS MAN THAT YOU ARE MINDFUL OF HIM, THE SON OF MAN
THAT YOU CARE FOR HIM?
YOU MADE HIM A LITTLE LOWER THAN THE HEAVENLY BEINGS
AND CROWNED HIM WITH GLORY AND HONOR.
YOU MADE HIM RULER OVER THE WORKS OF YOUR HANDS;
YOU PUT EVERYTHING UNDER HIS FEET: ALL FLOCKS AND HERDS,
AND THE BEASTS OF THE FIELD,
THE BIRDS OF THE AIR, AND THE FISH OF THE SEA, ALL THAT
SWIM THE PATHS OF THE SEAS.
LORD, OUR LORD, HOW MAJESTIC IS YOUR NAME IN ALL THE EARTH!

Psalm 8:3-9

CHAPTER 6

CHOOSE UNSELFISHNESS

LOVE IS NOT SELF-SEEKING.

1 Corinthians 13:5b

Kids need superheroes in their lives. Who is your child's superhero? Not Batman or Superman, but real-life superheroes to walk alongside them on the journey. Lori and I declare it's *you*! You are the hero that takes a special interest in your child, helping him to become all that he can be for the glory of God. Heroes all share a certain quality. No, not colored tights. Unselfishness. That's the common denominator.

Unselfishness brings relational satisfaction while selfishness spurs disputes. Selfish behaviors within a family can leave family members feeling neglected and unloved. When we take the time to fill the basic needs of our children, they feel loved. Living by the Golden Rule, do unto others as you'd have them do unto you (Matthew 7:12), demonstrates love, looking out for another's needs as you would your own. Unselfishness is outward focused. It causes us to step aside and place others front and center. Being thankful and knowing all blessings are from the Lord characterize unselfish living!

TURN MY HEART TOWARD YOUR STATUTES AND NOT TOWARD SELFISH GAIN.

Psalm 119:36

REFLECT

Who was your superhero as a child?

What is your first impulse, to meet another's need or your own? (Don't you hate some of these questions?)

Do you bow to the throne of God, or are you sitting on it? (Sometimes I feel the slivers.)

RELATE

Fill in the blanks for the six basic needs.

GOD'S IMAGE	HUMAN NEED GENERATED
Rational (God is logical, thinking)	_____
Volitional (God has a will, is powerful, and independent)	_____
_____ (God is relational in the Trinity)	Security/Belonging/Love
Emotional (God has feeling)	_____, _____
Spiritual (God is spirit)	Spiritual

Refocus

How can your family live out the Golden Rule in Matthew 7:12: "Do to others what you would have them do to you"?

Take a careful look at your family calendar. Even if the activities are good, is your family too busy? How can you prioritize?

Pray Hebrews 13:16 over your child.

> Lord, help (child's name) not to forget to do good and to share with others, for with such sacrifices God is pleased. Amen.

For where your treasure is, there your heart will be also.

Matthew 6:21

CHAPTER 7

CHOOSE PEACE

LOVE ... IS NOT EASILY ANGERED.

1 Corinthians 13:5c

If love is not easily angered, why do our children frustrate us like they do? Being angry with a child's oppositional behavior is not the problem. The issue lies in how we respond. Scripture lays out the folly of acting in anger: "A fool gives full vent to his anger" (Proverbs 29:11a). "A fool shows his annoyance at once" (Proverbs 12:16a). "A fool is hotheaded and reckless" (Proverbs 14:16b). Anger needs to be examined closely.

As parents, we can choose to respond in love. Our children learn from our reactions and will mirror them. Anger is a secondary emotion triggered by a primary emotion such as frustration, annoyance, or even being hurried. We have a choice to make when we feel anger rising in us. React in anger or choose peace.

TURN FROM EVIL AND DO GOOD; SEEK PEACE AND PURSUE IT.

Psalm 34:14

Reflect

How was anger handled in your family when you were a child?

How do you generally express your anger?

How does your child express his anger?

RELATE

"Encourage cooperation by being _____ and _____ in your directions and expectations."

What are your hot spots? Develop a rage interrupter that can be quickly and easily implemented to help you gain control when you're angry.

Have you been hijacked by a temper tantrum? What strategies can you use to avoid or reduce your child's tantrums in the future?

REFOCUS

How can James 1:19-20 assist you in creating a more peaceful home? "My dear brothers, take note of this: Everyone should be quick to listen, slow to speak and slow to become angry, for man's anger does not bring about the righteous life that God desires."

Read through the *A–Zs of Cooperative Interaction* found in the appendix of *The 1 Corinthians 13 Parent: Raising Little Kids with Big Love* to determine which techniques would work best for you and your children.

PRAY GALATIANS 5:22-23 FOR YOUR CHILD.

Lord Jesus, fill (child's name) with the fruit of the Spirit: love, joy, peace, patience, kindness, goodness, faithfulness, gentleness and self-control.
Amen.

BETTER A DRY CRUST WITH PEACE AND QUIET THAN A HOUSE FULL OF FEASTING, WITH STRIFE.

Proverbs 17:1

CHAPTER 8

CHOOSE FORGIVENESS

LOVE ... KEEPS NO RECORD OF WRONGS.

1 Corinthians 13:5d

Grudges, unforgiveness, and guilt drag a person down. Bitterness can affect the whole family. When old grievances are dredged up, the pain is prolonged. There is freedom in forgiving and forgetting. God forgives us as far as the east is from the west (Psalm 103:12). It's hard to do, yet that is our model. Hanging onto our bitter baggage wears us out.

How would you describe your home? Is it a place filled with grace and forgiveness or one where only perfection is tolerated and grudges are held? A forgiving atmosphere permeates the home with peace. We want our children to understand fully the depth of forgiveness God has given to us in Jesus. Begin at home by teaching your children to forgive honestly and to be humbly forgiven. As the parent be willing to admit your mistakes and ask for forgiveness. Put restitution and repentance into play in your family.

THEREFORE, MY BROTHERS, I WANT YOU TO KNOW THAT THROUGH JESUS THE FORGIVENESS OF SINS IS PROCLAIMED TO YOU.

Acts 13:38

REFLECT

What grudges or record of wrongs are you still holding?

What is the importance of asking for forgiveness instead of just apologizing?

Whom do you need to forgive? For what do you need to be forgiven?

RELATE

What tempts you? What tempts your children?

When frustrated, stressed, or annoyed, what bad habits do you typically slip into? How do you intend to change?

Have you felt the freedom in forgiving or being forgiven?

Refocus

Mediate on Psalm 139:23-24: "Search me, O God, and know my heart; test me and know my anxious thoughts. See if there is any offensive way in me, and lead me in the way everlasting." Pray for the Lord to reveal your offenses and guide you in overcoming each of them.

The next time you are in a position of needing to forgive, rather than focusing on why, consider the situation as a learning experience. Ask yourself, "How can I respond in a way that honors God?"

Pray Paul's words written in Acts 26:18.

Lord Jesus, open (child's name) eyes and turn him from darkness to light, and from the power of Satan to God, so that (child's name) may receive forgiveness of sins and a place among those who are sanctified in faith in you.
Amen.

Be kind and compassionate to one another,
forgiving each other,
just as in Christ God forgave you.

Ephesians 4:32

CHAPTER 9

CHOOSE GOODNESS

LOVE DOES NOT DELIGHT IN EVIL.

1 Corinthians 13:6a

Bad habits are hard to break. As Christians we have a secret weapon: the Holy Spirit. He has the strength to free us from sinful chains. We don't always tap into that power. There are instances when we are unfocused or distracted and we fall into the bad habits of complacency and ungodly compromise. Unfortunately, this behavior affects our children in negative ways.

Make a decision to turn from bad behavior to godly actions. Pray for the Holy Spirit to guide you. Encourage desirable traits in your children. State your expectations clearly. Pray for your child to be filled to the brim with attributes that will glorify God.

ANSWER ME, LORD, OUT OF THE GOODNESS OF YOUR LOVE; IN YOUR GREAT MERCY TURN TO ME.

Psalm 69:16

REFLECT

What bad habits have you developed that you are passing on to your children (swearing, coveting, impatience)?

Where have you compromised, viewing the sin in your life as acceptable or even respectable?

How does your child respond to a mistake? Does he blame others?

RELATE

What are examples of the three stages of conscience development?

1. Responding to stimuli   _____

2. Obedience training   _____

3. Discernment development   _____

Why is "Why?" a good question for a child to ask and a parent to answer?

What strategies will you use to stop tattling?

REFOCUS

Identify three undesirable character traits in your child. List the opposing desirable characteristics to pray for using the replacement technique.

1._____ replace with _____

2._____ replace with _____

3._____ replace with _____

What is H.A.L.T.?

H - _____

A - _____

L - _____

T - _____

Why is it important to identify triggers?

PRAY FOR THE ATTRIBUTES IN 2 PETER 1:5 TO BE INSTILLED IN YOUR CHILD.

Lord, add to (child's name) faith, goodness; and to goodness,
knowledge; and to knowledge, self-control; and to self-control,
perseverance; and to perseverance, godliness; and to godliness,
brotherly kindness; and to brotherly kindness, love.
Amen.

WITH THIS IN MIND, WE CONSTANTLY PRAY FOR YOU, THAT OUR
GOD MAY COUNT YOU WORTHY OF HIS CALLING,
AND THAT BY HIS POWER HE MAY FULFILL EVERY GOOD PURPOSE
OF YOURS AND EVERY ACT PROMPTED BY YOUR FAITH.

2 Thessalonians 1:11

CHAPTER 10

CHOOSE TRUTH

LOVE REJOICES WITH THE TRUTH.

1 Corinthians 13:6b

Cultural truth is quicksand. Biblical truth is solid ground. Where do you want to stand? As Christian parents we are the spiritual leaders in the home, using the Word of God to lead our kids to solid ground.

Plan intentional faith-formation lessons for your children. Spontaneously show them the glory of God. Decide now to leave a legacy of faith for your children. Devise a plan. You are the most important source of biblical teaching for your child. Make the most of every day. What you instill in your child today will add to his foundation of faith for tomorrow.

THE LORD IS NEAR TO ALL WHO CALL ON HIM, TO ALL WHO CALL ON HIM IN TRUTH.
Psalm 145:18

REFLECT
Who is the spiritual leader in your home?

What is your definition of absolute truth?

To whom do you turn in a crisis?

RELATE

List examples of intentional and spontaneous faith-filled teaching times.

Intentional:

Spontaneous:

Devise a plan to implement intentional and spontaneous faith-filled experiences.

Define P.O.W.W. and give an example of each.

P_____   _____

Other Christians   _____

Worship   _____

W_____   _____

Refocus

Use the three parenting tips presented in Chapter 10 of *Raising Little Kids with Big Love* to assist you in leaving a legacy of faith.

How does your home reflect your family's faith to visitors?

Pray Psalm 25:4 for your child.

Jesus, show (child's name) your ways. O LORD, teach (child's name) your paths; guide (child's name) in your truth and teach (child's name), for you are God (child's name) Savior, and (child's name) hope is in you all day long.
Amen.

JESUS ANSWERED, "I AM THE WAY AND THE TRUTH AND THE LIFE. NO ONE COMES TO THE FATHER EXCEPT THROUGH ME."

John 14:6

CHAPTER 11

CHOOSE TO PROTECT

LOVE ALWAYS PROTECTS.

1 Corinthians 13:7a

Parents of toddlers and youngsters spend a lot of time protecting their children. From physical hazards of falling to emotional trauma of being left out, parents are the protectors. Boundaries are created by family rules, set in place to safeguard children. Parents are the child's first line of defense for the protection of body, mind, and spirit.

By not compromising on media guidelines, nonnegotiable rules, and family values we reveal a desire to protect our children, no matter what. Allowing kids to experience natural consequences gives them real-life learning and practice in decision-making. Encouraging youngsters, where appropriate, to advocate for themselves helps them realize they are capable. Each child is beautifully and wonderfully made, to be protected and treasured.

BUT LET ALL WHO TAKE REFUGE IN YOU BE GLAD; LET THEM EVER SING FOR JOY. SPREAD YOUR PROTECTION OVER THEM, THAT THOSE WHO LOVE YOUR NAME MAY REJOICE IN YOU.

Psalm 5:11

REFLECT

As a child, did your family holiday traditions reflect your family's faith? Do they now?

Where have you compromised your family's values to help your child fit in with his friends?

When have you allowed your child to experience natural consequences for his actions?

RELATE

"_____ and guidelines provide _____ for children that in turn give them a sense of _____."

What are the nonnegotiable safety rules in your family?

How does the amount and type of protection you provide change as your child matures? How will the four positive parenting styles help you in this transition?

REFOCUS

How can the words in Psalm 101:3 ("I will set no vile thing before my eyes") assist you in determining your family's media guidelines?

Parents need to protect not hover, love not smother. In what circumstances can you encourage your child to be his own advocate?

PRAY FOR YOUR CHILD USING PSALM 28:6.

> Praise be to the Lord for your have heard (child's name) cry for mercy. The Lord is (child's name) strength and (child's name) shield; (child's name) trusts in you, and (child's name) is helped. (Child's name) heart leaps for joy and (child's name) will give thanks to you in song. Amen.

MAY THE LORD ANSWER YOU WHEN YOU ARE IN DISTRESS; MAY THE NAME OF THE GOD OF JACOB PROTECT YOU.

Psalm 20:1

CHAPTER 12

CHOOSE TO TRUST

LOVE ALWAYS TRUSTS.

1 Corinthians 13:7b

Trust is a valuable commodity in families. To be trustworthy is godly. To be able to wholeheartedly trust another person is a gift. Keeping promises teaches children that words matter and integrity counts. In providing a trusting environment for children, we give them the chance to learn to trust their heavenly Father. Trust is a loving component in families. Trusting in God is crucial. "Those who know your name will trust in you, for you, LORD, have never forsaken those who seek you" (Psalm 9:10).

Let's delve deeper into this attribute. Lies can quickly demolish the foundation of trust we build with our children. So focus on the truth, protecting the relationship by being a person worthy of trust. When children trust their parents, they are more comfortable coming to them with questions and for help in a variety of situations. Trust can relieve fears and refresh the soul.

THE LAW OF THE LORD IS PERFECT, REVIVING THE SOUL.
THE STATUTES OF THE LORD ARE TRUSTWORTHY,
MAKING WISE THE SIMPLE.

Psalm 19:7

REFLECT

As a child, were the adults in your life trustworthy?

How often do you tell little white lies or embellish stories?

What personal fears have you passed on to your child?

RELATE

What are the three reasons children tell lies? Define the lie.

1. _____ _____

2. _____ _____

3. _____ _____

How will increasing your trustworthiness provide security for your child?

What are a few ideas you can use to assist your child with separation anxiety?

Refocus

Think of a typical scenario in which your child has lied. How can you use a mixture of Chum and Consultant techniques to address the lie?

Use a penny as a tangible reference for the trustworthiness of God. Show it to your child. Place one in his pocket as a reminder. (Caution: Don't use this technique if your child is still putting items in his mouth.)

Pray the words of Psalm 143:8 for your child.

Lord, let the morning bring (child's name) word of your unfailing love, for (child's name) has put his/her trust in you. Show (child's name) the way (he/she) should go, for you (child's name) lifts up (his/her) soul.

Amen.

You will keep in perfect peace him whose mind
is steadfast, because he trusts in you.
Trust in the Lord forever, for the Lord, the Lord,
is the Rock eternal.

Isaiah 26:3-4

CHAPTER 13

CHOOSE TO HOPE

LOVE ALWAYS HOPES.

1 Corinthians 13:7c

Children turn to mom and dad for hope and encouragement in the storms of life. During these times we can show our kids how to look to God in crises. Because our heavenly Father is faithful and trustworthy, our hope can be restored. Jesus reassures us in John 14:1, "Do not let your hearts be troubled. Trust in God; trust also in me." He is trustworthy!

Let's dig deep into finding hope in the midst of grief, depression, and disappointment. Hope inspires courage. We can be courageous, even in our suffering, because we belong to Jesus. This is valuable for children to know and remember in the difficult times. The Lord's trustworthiness and faithfulness provide hope for His children.

BUT THE NEEDY WILL NOT ALWAYS BE FORGOTTEN,
NOR THE HOPE OF THE AFFLICTED EVER PERISH.

Psalm 9:18

REFLECT

Who do you typically turn to when life gets difficult?

Have you ever lived vicariously through your child? If so, when?

Does your child give up easily? Why or why not?

RELATE

What are some ways to foster a hope-filled attitude in your child?

What are some creative ways you can act as your child's advocate for his special needs?

How can you encourage your child to be a bearer of hope?

REFOCUS

What out-of-the-box behavior could create hope in your child?

"A family focused on _____ with a _____ attitude will tenaciously withstand storms and will flourish."

PRAY PSALM 33:22 FOR YOUR CHILD.

May your unfailing love rest upon (child's name), O Lord, even as (child's name) puts (child's name) hope in you. Amen.

**BE STRONG AND LET YOUR HEART TAKE HEART,
ALL YOU WHO HOPE IN THE LORD.**

Psalm 31:24

CHAPTER 14

CHOOSE TENACITY

LOVE ALWAYS PERSEVERES.
1 Corinthians 13:7d

The Bible is filled with stories of those who have overcome adversity with God's help. Persevering has purpose when we understand God has good and prosperous plans for His children. He will give us hope and a future (see Jeremiah 29:11). Even when Daniel was in the lion's den, God did great things (see Daniel 6). He can do great things for you, too.

Instilling perseverance in children will aid them when facing life's disappointments. Tenacity is a skill and a frame of mind. Praise your child for a job well done. Correct him when he needs correcting. Support his efforts and encourage his success in school and extracurricular activities. Walk with him when he is grieving. Read and talk about biblical accounts of God's amazing provision in hopeless situations. God is with your child, and only the Lord possesses the power to do the impossible. Trust God and act with tenacity.

NOT ONLY SO, BUT WE ALSO REJOICE IN OUR SUFFERINGS, BECAUSE WE KNOW THAT SUFFERING PRODUCES PERSEVERANCE; PERSEVERANCE, CHARACTER; AND CHARACTER, HOPE.

Romans 5:3-4

REFLECT

As a child, were you built up with sincere or insincere praise?

Are you generally tenacious or do you give up easily?

How do you explain death to your child?

RELATE

If your child is struggling with a new skill, how can you break the task into smaller parts to encourage success?

Commitment is a characteristic of being tenacious. How do you respond when your child wants to quit an activity rather than see it through?

What are some techniques for assisting your child in handling grief?

REFOCUS

Look up the following biblical accounts of God's intervention on behalf of his children. What can you apply to your own life or your child's?

Exodus 14

Daniel 6

1 Samuel 17

"_____ and _____ are the direct results of hope and perseverance in the midst of trials."

PRAY THE WORDS OF HEBREWS 12:1 OVER YOUR CHILD.

Therefore since (child's name) is surrounded by such a great cloud of witnesses, let (child's name) throw off everything that hinders and the sin that so easily entangles, and let (child's name) run with perseverance the race marked out for him/her.
Amen.

YOU NEED TO PERSEVERE SO THAT WHEN YOU HAVE DONE THE WILL OF GOD, YOU WILL RECEIVE WHAT HE HAS PROMISED.

Hebrews 10:36

CONCLUSION

CHOOSE TO FLOURISH

LOVE NEVER FAILS.

1 Corinthians 13:8

"And now these three remain: faith, hope and love. But the greatest of these is love" (1 Corinthians 13:13). Love is the greatest of all attributes. Perfect love is found in Jesus Christ alone. John tells us, "This is love: not that we loved God, but that he loved us and sent his Son as an atoning sacrifice for our sins" (1 John 4:10). Leading our children to the cross takes time, effort, and a lot of prayer. Each time there is a new believer "there is rejoicing in the presence of the angels of God over one sinner who repents" (Luke 15:10b). What a gift!

Paul writes, "When I was a child I talked like a child, thought like a child, I reasoned like a child. When I became a man I put childish ways behind me" (1 Corinthians 13:1). As parents, we are called to put prior poor parenting practices and childish ways behind us. Retake the *Parent Assessment* beginning on the next page. Think about what you've learned and are already implementing in your family.

Parent Assessment

As you read each statement below, give it a number that corresponds to how well you believe you do or how much you agree with each item. Please use your first impression.

1. Not Yet
2. Just Started
3. Halfway There
4. Mostly Developed
5. In Place

_____I adjust my discipline techniques according to my child's age, stage, and personality.

_____I avoid speaking for my child.

_____Each family member is strongly committed to the family.

_____I encourage sibling relationships.

_____I resist the urge to compare one child to another.

_____I effectively deal with undesirable behavior, like lying or stealing.

_____Respect permeates the home.

_____Responsibilities are shared.

_____I don't punish my children because of my anger.

_____My family shares an attitude of forgiveness.

_____I attempt to understand the reasons behind my child's behavior.

_____My family supports one another in difficult times.

_____I arm my children with strategies to help during tempting moments.

_____Family mealtimes are a priority.

_____I teach my children right from wrong using God's Word, the Bible.

_____A common bond of faith is important in my family.

_____I am able to work effectively with my child's teachers.

_____Appreciation for one another is demonstrated.

_____Clear family guidelines for technology and media are stated.

_____Screen time (computer, TV, iPod, etc.) is limited in our home.

_____Priorities are clearly defined.

_____There's a sense of humor and play in the home.

_____Crises are dealt with by turning to God and family members for support.

_____Leisure time is spent together as a family.

_____My family believes each person is created for a purpose.

How did you do after reading *The 1 Corinthians 13 Parent: Raising Little Kids with Big Love* and completing the study guide? We hope you are making some changes with the suggested strategies. Which areas do you still need to focus on improving?

Pray and make a plan.

Commit to the Lord whatever you do, and your plans will succeed (Proverbs 16:3).

Love Is

Love is patient, love is kind—a decision.

It does not envy, it does not boast, it is not proud—an attitude.

It is not rude, it is not self-seeking—outward focus.

It is not easily angered, it keeps no record of wrongs—self-control.

Love does not delight in evil but rejoices with the truth—a heavenly perspective.

It always protects, always trusts, always hopes—an action.

It always perseveres, Love never fails—a commitment.

The greatest of these is love—ultimate strength.

REFLECT

Is Jesus Christ your Lord and Savior? "He is the stone you builders rejected, which has become the capstone. Salvation is found in no one else, for there is no other name under heaven given to men by which we must be saved" (Acts 4:11-12).

RELATE

Describe B.R.E.A.T.H. as it relates to every individual having value in the eyes of God.

B =

R =

E =

A =

T =

H =

What are the five basic principles for Christian living?

_____ _____.

Love _____ as you love yourself.

Do unto others as you would have them do unto you.

_____ as you have been forgiven.

Have an _____ of _____.

How has the study of *The 1 Corinthians 13 Parent: Raising Little Kids with Big Love* encouraged and motivated you on your parenting journey? We would love to hear your feedback. Connect with Becky at www.beckydanielson.com or with Lori at www.loriwildenberg.com.

REFOCUS

Use the ABCs when leading your children to Jesus.

A - Ask Jesus to forgive your sins.

B - Believe in your heart God raised Jesus from the dead.

C - Confess with your mouth, Jesus is Lord.

How will your faith outlive you?

Make a commitment to use the Bible daily as a parenting tool.

FOR THE WORD OF GOD IS LIVING AND ACTIVE. SHARPER THAN ANY DOUBLE-EDGED SWORD, IT PENETRATES EVEN TO DIVIDING SOUL AND SPIRIT, JOINTS AND MARROW; IT JUDGES THE THOUGHTS AND ATTITUDES OF THE HEART.

Hebrews 4:12

Lori and I have a mission statement for our ministry: *to equip and encourage parents with God's Word.* The Bible is your guide. Use it every day. Rely on it always. Luke recorded Jesus' words, "Blessed rather are those who hear the word of God and obey it" (Luke 11:28).

May God bless your family abundantly as you continue to study the Bible for guidance as you raise your children with a heavenly perspective. His Word is *the* parenting handbook, and 1 Corinthians 13 shows God's *most excellent way* to love (1 Corinthians 12:31).

Every word of God is flawless;
he is a shield to those who take refuge in him.

Proverbs 30:5

ANSWER KEY

While most questions in this supplemental manual are personal, others require a specific response. For those particular questions, we have provided the answers.

INTRODUCTION

1 = Coach

2 = Chum

3 = Controller

4 = Clueless

5 = Consultant

6 = Checked Out

CHAPTER 3

"True contentment with <u>who</u> one is and with <u>what</u> one has creates joyful satisfaction."

The six steps to disengage before sibling squabbles escalate are:

1. Separate siblings.
2. Ask each child to come up with a positive solution to the dispute.
3. Have each child explain the plan he has devised.
4. Encourage compromise, incorporating parts of both plans.
5. Have the kids present their plan to the parent.
6. Allow the kids to come to a final resolution and implement their plan.

CHAPTER 5

"If obedience is desired, don't ask a <u>question</u>, don't whine, and don't bargain. Issue a <u>statement</u> and be ready to <u>move</u>."

What are the steps for gaining cooperation?

1. <u>State expectations</u> prior to an event. This is positive prevention. "Hang onto the cart when we are in the grocery store" (Controller).

2. <u>Train</u> while the event is occurring and mention the family value to be reinforced. "Remember, hang onto the cart while we are in the store so we can stick together" (Controller/Coach).

3. <u>Retrain with a stated consequence</u> if the child isn't obeying. "Hang on or you'll have to get in the cart. To be safe we stick together" (Controller).

4. <u>Follow through</u> with the stated consequence if the child doesn't obey the instruction. "In the cart you go. This will keep you safe" (Controller).

5. <u>Punishment</u> is the final step. Parent's choice. Try to make it fit the crime.

CHAPTER 6

Fill in the blanks for the six basic needs.

GOD'S IMAGE	HUMAN NEED GENERATED
Rational (God is logical, thinking)	Respect
Volitional (God has a will, is powerful, and independent)	Freedom
Volitional (God is relational in the Trinity)	Security/Belonging/Love
Emotional (God has emotion)	Joy, Fun
Spiritual (God is spirit)	Spiritual

CHAPTER 7

Encourage cooperation by being <u>clear</u> and <u>concise</u> with directions and expectations.

Chapter 9

What are examples of the three stages of conscience development? (Your answers may be slightly different.)

1. Responding to stimuli   <u>Being fed when hungry.</u>

2. Obedience training   <u>Waiting to be served.</u>

3. Discernment development   <u>Gently taking a cookie from Mom's hand rather than snatching it.</u>

What is H.A.L.T., and why are these triggers valuable when identified?

H - <u>Hungry</u>

A - <u>Angry</u>

L - <u>Lonely</u>

T - <u>Tired</u>

<u>These are weak moments, times when the child is most likely to behave badly.</u>

Chapter 10

Define P.O.W.W. and give an example of each.

<u>Prayer</u>   <u>Praying Scripture for your child</u>

Other Christians   <u>Christian friends</u>

Worship   <u>Belonging to a church, a body of believers</u>

<u>Word</u>   <u>Sharing Bible stories</u>

Chapter 11

"<u>Rules</u> and guidelines provide <u>boundaries</u> for children that in turn give them a sense of <u>security</u>."

Chapter 12

What are the three reasons children tell lies? Define the lie.

      1. <u>Attention</u>   <u>Generally fantasy, to attract attention.</u>

      2. <u>Acceptance</u>   <u>To belong or feel secure.</u>

      3. <u>Avoidance</u>   <u>To keep oneself out of trouble; by omission (leaving out the truth) or commission (boldface lie)</u>

Chapter 13

"A family focused on <u>Christ</u> with a <u>hopeful</u> attitude will tenaciously withstand storms and will flourish."

Chapter 14

"<u>Resiliency</u> and <u>determination</u> are the direct results of hope and perseverance in the midst of trials."

Conclusion

Describe B.R.E.A.T.H. as it relates to every individual having value in the eyes of God.

      B = Bent—know and study your child.

      R = Rejoice in his successes.

      E = Express empathy for the challenges.

      A = Avoid comparisons with siblings.

      T = Talents are appreciated.

      H = Has purpose.

What are the five basic principles for Christian living?

> <u>Love</u> <u>God</u>.

> Love <u>others</u> as you love yourself.

> Do unto others as you would have them do unto you.

> <u>Forgive</u> as you have been forgiven.

> Have an <u>attitude</u> of <u>gratitude</u>.

About the Authors

Lori Wildenberg

Lori Wildenberg knows full well the struggles a parent with little kids experiences. At one point, Lori had four kids, ages five and under! Lori is passionate about coming alongside parents to encourage, empower, strengthen, and support them. She communicates effectively with transparency, warmth, and gentle humor. Her straightforward, realistic approach engages her audience and assists moms and dads in their quest to parent well. Lori has more than twenty-five years' experience working with parents and kids in both secular and faith-based settings. She is a licensed parent and family educator who meets parents where they are and helps them get to where they want to go. Lori openly shares her personal and professional experience using a "been there, done that" approach. Her parenting philosophy is focused on developing a child's heart and character; this sets her apart from many other parenting voices out there. Lori and her ministry partner, Becky Danielson, are founders of *1 Corinthians 13 Parenting*. Together they have authored three faith-based parenting books, including the second *1 Corinthians 13 Parent book, Raising Big Kids with Supernatural Love*. Lori is also a mentor mom with The M.O.M. Initiative and writes curriculum for and trains teachers at the Professional Learning Board.

The Wildenbergs live in the foothills of the Rocky Mountains. A perfect day in Lori's world is hiking with her husband, Tom, four kids, and labradoodle.

Becky Danielson, M.Ed.

Becky Danielson's favorite title is Mom. She and her husband, Scott, have two active and fun-loving teenage boys. She is a licensed Parent and Family educator and co-founder of *1 Corinthians 13 Parenting* with her ministry partner, Lori Wildenberg. Above all she is a follower of Jesus Christ.

Becky has spent a lot of time in school as a learner, teacher, and volunteer. After attending Gustavus Adolphus College for her Bachelor's degree (K-6 Education, Early Childhood Education), she received her Master's degree from St. Mary's University, and a license in Parent and Family Education from Crown College.

Before becoming a stay-at-home-mom, she taught kindergarten and first grade. The birth of her two boys changed her life and career completely. Sharing God's Word to equip and encourage families has become Becky's passion. The parents she works with, either in a large group setting or one-on-one mentoring, find her warm, honest, and supportive. Her ideas and parenting tips are practical, encouraging, and applicable. Becky candidly shares her life as a Christian wife, mom, and educator. Along with co-authoring the *1 Corinthians 13 Parent books*, Becky contributes to *Hooray for Family*, a print and online magazine, *The Pearl Girls*, and *Faith Village*.

When she's not writing or meeting with moms and dads, Becky can be found in her kitchen garden, reading, or on an adventure with her Danielson men!

CONNECT WITH 1 CORINTHIANS 13 PARENTING AT

WWW.1CORINTHIANS13PARENTING.COM

LORI is available for speaking, parent consulting, and teacher in-service training. Contact her at www.loriwildenberg.com or www.1Corinthians13Parenting.com.

Connect with BECKY at www.beckydanielson.com or www.1Corinthians13Parenting.com to speak at your next event or for parent mentoring.

Made in the USA
Las Vegas, NV
09 May 2022